Is it not you? Indeed, you are our glory and joy.

I Thessalonians 2:19-20

MINISTRY IS
WAY TOO GOOD
NOT TO ENJOY IT

Books by Tim Barker

Anticipating the Return of Christ

At Your Feet

Called Camp 2025

Discovering God in the Secret Places

End Times

God's Revelation and Your Future

It's Not All About Sitting at the Head Table

Mighty Men of Courage from the Bible

My Jesus Journey

My Jesus Journey: Crescendo

My Jesus Journey: Glissando

My Jesus Journey: Rhapsody

Names of God

Open Doors

One. Less. Stone.

Our Privilege of Joy

Reflecting Christ Through the Fruit of the Spirit

The Age of Uncertainty

The Authentic Christian: Revealing Christ through the Fruit of the Spirit

The Call of Ephesians

The Lord with Us

The Night Heaven Broke Its Silence

The Twelve: Taking Up the Mantle of Christ

The Vision of Nehemiah: God's Plan for Righteous Living

Truth, Love & Redemption: The Holy Spirit for Today

Unified Church

Your Invitation to Christ

MINISTRY IS
WAY TOO GOOD
NOT TO ENJOY IT

Tim R. Barker, D. Min.

Network Pastor/Superintendent
South Texas Ministry Network

MINISTRY IS WAY TOO GOOD NOT TO
ENJOY IT
By Tim Barker

1st ed.

ISBN: 979-8-9924875-8-9

DEDICATION

In honor of Pastor Claude Johnson, a faithful Presbyter and dedicated leader who blessed and guided me during my early years of ministry.

I am forever grateful.

PREFACE

We don't hear much taught about the joy of ministry.

The responsibility, yes. Showing up on time, that too. Being available around the clock ... hospital duty ... three services a week ... are you tired already?

The other side of ministry is the joy that leads ministers to jump on board and lead people with the Gospel message.

One of the most powerful passages regarding the joy of ministry is found in 1 Thessalonians 2:19–20, where the Apostle Paul receives joy from those under his ministry:

> *"For what is our hope, our joy, or the crown in which we will glory in the presence of our Lord Jesus when he comes? Is it not you? Indeed, you are our glory and joy."*

Joy also comes when we witness growth as Paul did in Philippians 1:4. His joy came from interceding for others.

"In all my prayers for all of you, I always pray with joy."

2 Corinthians 7:4 tells us that the joy of ministry can coexist with suffering.

"I am overflowing with joy in all our afflictions."

In Philippians 2:17–18, Paul expresses joy even in the prospect of being *"poured out like a drink offering"* for the service of others' faith. He found joy in the process of selfless service.

Other sources of joy can come from our reward. In the Parable of the Talents (Matt. 25:21), the faithful servant is told, *"Well done, good and faithful servant... Enter into the joy of your master."*

John 4:36–38 explains that both the one who sows the seed and the one who reaps the harvest can rejoice together in the work of God.

Psalm 100:2 commands believers to *"Serve the Lord with gladness; come before His presence with joyful songs."*

For those feeling the weight of ministry, Hebrews 13:17 encourages leaders to watch over souls *"with joy and not with groaning,"* noting that joyful leadership is an advantage for the entire body of Christ.

This book is designed as a mirror. If you see yourself in it, take heart. God wants to return His joy to you.

TABLE OF CONTENTS

INTRODUCTION

Ministry is one of the most exciting life choices I can imagine.

Sharing the Gospel. Ministering while leading in song. Inviting the lost to find hope, peace, and reconciliation though Christ.

Ministry has been my driving force since I was in college. Yes, there have been a few bumps in my "Jesus Journey," but the God I serve has picked me up each time and set my feet back on this ministry journey that has served me so well.

Let me share with you the reason for this book:

Ministry is as close as we can get to being the hand of Christ to the people who walk on this earth with us. It's a thrilling life of connection to the Father, the Son, and the Holy Spirit, and we also get the icing on the cake, a direct connection to the wonderful people who share this "Jesus Journey" with us.

How amazing is that?

Yet, during my bumpy times, it hasn't always felt joyous. My relationship with God never changed, but my joy in my ministry did.

That's not what God intends for us. That's not His ministry blessing ... his gift of enthusiasm and fulfillment in doing His work on this earth.

Each time a bump in my journey has robbed me of my joy, I've had to reconnect with that joy. The thing is that when your joy has been stolen by the busyness and repetitive nature of ministry, you don't even know it's gone.

Life becomes the new normal.

The God of Bethlehem still speaks today. The God of Moses is still performing miracles. Joy still flows from our hearts when we let God inside the shell of the "new normal" that tries so hard to steal our joy from us.

I want to shatter the new normal and bring you back to where God wants you to be ... wrapped in, coddled by, and overwhelmed with the joy you once knew when ministry was fresh to you.

Your joy (or the lack of it) bleeds into your congregation with every hand you shake, every message you give, and every smile you return.

If you have joy, your congregation will also have joy. That's how ministry works.

The Lion of Judah is still a force to be reckoned with. While He came as a lamb, He is here today as a mighty rushing river. It's time to jump in and get covered by His joy.

You chose ministry for a reason. It is way too good not to enjoy it. Let's reconnect with the joy that makes it all worthwhile.

Tim

THE QUIET DANGER NO ONE WARNED YOU ABOUT

No one warned you about this part of ministry.

They warned you about *temptation*.
They warned you about *criticism*.
They warned you about *false doctrine, burnout, and betrayal*.

But almost no one warned you about the slow erosion of joy.

Because it doesn't arrive violently.
It doesn't announce itself loudly.
It doesn't come with moral failure or public collapse.

It arrives quietly—disguised as faithfulness.

You're still preaching.
  Still praying.
  Still showing up.
  Still carrying the weight.

And that's why it's so dangerous.

There is a form of spiritual drift that doesn't pull you away from God—it pulls the delight out of obedience. You don't stop loving God. You don't stop believing the Word. You simply stop enjoying the very thing God once lit your soul on fire to do.

This is the danger no one warned you about.

THE MOST DANGEROUS DRIFT IS NOT SIN—IT IS NUMBNESS

Most leaders don't walk away because they stop believing.

They walk away because they stop *feeling alive*.

Somewhere along the way:

- Calling turns into carrying
- Passion turns into pressure
- Ministry turns into maintenance

You don't quit.
You don't rebel.
You just endure.

And endurance without joy will hollow out even the strongest soul.

There is a tragic irony in ministry:

You can spend your life helping others encounter

God while quietly drifting from the joy of encountering Him yourself.

This is not rebellion.

This is erosion.

And erosion happens slowly.

HOW JOY LEAKS OUT OF GOOD LEADERS

Joy rarely leaves all at once.

It leaks.

It leaks through:

- *Unprocessed disappointment*
- *Accumulated fatigue*
- *Constant urgency*
- *Emotional isolation*
- *The pressure to always be "okay"*

Every leader knows this moment:

You're still effective—*but you're not fulfilled.*
You're still anointed—*but you're tired in places oil doesn't reach.*
You're still faithful—*but something feels thin.*

You tell yourself, *"This is just the season."*
You say, *"It'll get better after this push."*
You promise yourself rest that keeps getting

postponed.

But joy is not restored by postponement.

It is restored by presence.

WHEN FAITHFULNESS BECOMES A HIDING PLACE

Here's the danger: *faithfulness can hide joylessness.*

Because everyone sees your consistency—*but no one sees your interior weariness.*

You keep preaching because it's what you do.
You keep leading because people depend on you.
You keep smiling because leaders aren't supposed to be discouraged.

And slowly, subtly, ministry becomes something you manage instead of something you marvel at.

You no longer wake up grateful—*you wake up responsible.*

And responsibility without joy becomes resentment in disguise.

SCRIPTURE NEVER GLORIFIES JOYLESS OBEDIENCE

The Bible never praises hollow faithfulness.

David said, "In Your presence is fullness of joy."

Not partial joy.
Not occasional joy.

Fullness.

Nehemiah told weary builders, "The joy of the Lord is your strength."

Not discipline.
Not grit.

Joy.

Joy is not an accessory to obedience.
Joy is a byproduct of alignment.

When joy is gone, it's not because you stopped serving.

It's because something slipped out of alignment.

THE LIE THAT KEEPS LEADERS STUCK

Here's the lie many leaders believe but never say out loud:

"If I were more spiritual, I wouldn't feel this way."

So instead of addressing joy loss, you spiritualize it.
You normalize it.
You suppress it.

But God never asked you to bury joy. He asked you to bear fruit, and joy is part of that fruit.

Joylessness is not a sign of maturity. *It's a sign of neglect.*

A HOLY INTERRUPTION

Let me interrupt the narrative you've been telling yourself:

Ministry is not supposed to feel like a slow emotional death.

You were not called to *survive sermons.*
You were not called to *outlast people.*
You were not called to *endure God's work as if it were punishment.*

You were called to walk with God—**and walking with God has always been marked by joy**.

Not shallow happiness.
Not denial.
But deep, sustaining delight.

THE QUESTION THIS CHAPTER LEAVES YOU WITH

Before we go any further, you have to sit with this question:

When did joy quietly slip out of your calling— and why did no one notice?

And maybe more importantly:

Why did you decide it was normal?

God is not offended by that question.
He's inviting you to answer it with Him.

Because ministry is way too good—
    not to enjoy it.

2

WHEN CALLING TURNS INTO CARRYING

Calling is a gift.
Carrying is a weight.

Calling lifts you.
Carrying wears you down.

Most people never notice the difference—**until joy disappears.**

When God first called you, the weight didn't bother you. You carried responsibility with gratitude. You said yes with excitement. You felt the privilege of being chosen.

You knew the cost, but the joy outweighed it.

But somewhere along the journey, something shifted.

You didn't *stop being called.*
You didn't *stop being faithful.*

You didn't *stop obeying*.

You just started carrying more than you were meant to carry.

And joy was the first casualty.

THE SUBTLE SHIFT THAT DRAINS LEADERS

The shift from calling to carrying is rarely dramatic.

It doesn't come with *rebellion*.
It doesn't arrive with *cynicism*.
It sneaks in quietly—**under the banner of responsibility**.

You don't notice it at first.

You say yes because it's needed.
You step in because no one else will.
You absorb pressure because leaders are supposed to be strong.

And before long, **the thing that once energized you now exhausts you**.

You wake up thinking about *tasks* instead of *testimony*.
You pray about *logistics* instead of *longing*.
You lead from *obligation* instead of *overflow*.

The calling is still there—**but now it feels heavy**.

WHEN RESPONSIBILITY MULTIPLIES WITHOUT REPLENISHMENT

Here's the truth few leaders want to admit:

Responsibility multiplies faster than replenishment unless you guard it.

Every season adds something:

- More people
- More expectations
- More decisions
- More weight

But replenishment rarely happens automatically.

Calling brings grace.
Carrying requires boundaries.

And when boundaries aren't set, *leaders slowly become pack animals—**hauling loads God never assigned.***

Joy doesn't disappear because ministry is hard.
Joy disappears because weight accumulates unnoticed.

MOSES: CALLED BY GOD, CRUSHED BY CARRYING

Moses is one of the clearest pictures of this shift.

He was *unquestionably called.*
He was *undeniably anointed.*
He was *powerfully used.*

And yet—he collapsed.

Not because Israel was rebellious.
Not because God withdrew.
But because Moses was carrying the leadership alone.

Exodus tells us Moses sat from morning until evening judging the people. *Faithful. Available. Responsible.*

And completely unsustainable.

Jethro looked at Moses and said, *"What you are doing is not good."*

Not sinful.
Not immoral.
Not heretical.

Just not good.

Why? Because Moses was carrying more than his calling required.

And God didn't rebuke Moses for needing help.

God provided it.

Joy often returns not when we become more spiritual—*but when we become more honest about what we're carrying.*

THE MYTH OF "IF I DON'T, NO ONE WILL"

One of the most dangerous lies in ministry is this:

"If I don't do it, it won't get done."

That lie *sounds noble.*
It *feels responsible.*
But it quietly *replaces trust with control.*

God never designed ministry to depend entirely on one person's capacity.

When you believe everything rests on you:

- You stop delegating
- You stop resting
- You stop enjoying

Because joy requires trust—**and control suffocates trust.**

Calling says, *"God is at work."*
Carrying says, *"It's all on me."*

And when everything feels like it's on you, joy has no room to breathe.

WHEN WE START CARRYING EXPECTATIONS GOD NEVER GAVE

Not all weight comes from responsibility.

Some weight comes from expectation.

Expectations from:

- *People who don't understand the cost*
- *Systems that reward output over health*
- *Cultures that value visibility over vitality*
- *Your own inner critic that never rests*

You start carrying:

- *The need to be liked*
- *The pressure to succeed*
- *The fear of disappointing others*
- *The unspoken demand to always be available*

And none of those were ever part of your calling.

God called you to obedience—*not omnipresence.*
He called you to faithfulness—*not faultlessness.*

When you start carrying expectations God never gave, *joy will always suffer.*

WHY JESUS' YOKE MATTERS MORE THAN EVER

Jesus said His yoke was easy and His burden light.

A yoke means you are still pulling—*but you're not pulling alone.*

Here's the difference:

- Jesus' yoke aligns your pace with His.
- Self-imposed yokes force you to outrun grace.

Many leaders are exhausted not because ministry is demanding—**but because they are out of rhythm with Jesus**.

You're pulling—*but not beside Him.*
You're working—*but ahead of Him.*
You're serving—*but disconnected from Him.*

Joy is not lost because you're doing too much.
Joy is lost because you're doing it alone.

THE WEIGHT YOU WERE NEVER MEANT TO FEEL

Let me name some weights God never assigned you:

- *Fixing everyone*
- *Saving everyone*
- *Being everything*
- *Never disappointing anyone*

Those are messiah weights.

And there is only one Messiah.

When leaders try to carry what belongs to Christ, *joy always collapses.*

Relief comes when we release what was never ours.

A HOLY MOMENT OF HONESTY

Pause here.

Ask yourself—*not defensively*, but honestly:

What am I carrying right now that God never asked me to carry?

What responsibility started as obedience but turned into pressure?

What expectation am I afraid to put down?

Joy doesn't return through effort.
It returns through alignment.

When calling and carrying are realigned, *joy finds its way back.*

THE PROMISE THIS CHAPTER LEAVES YOU WITH

Jesus never called you to drag the weight of ministry without resurrection power.

He never asked you to trade joy for faithfulness.

If the calling feels heavier than it once did, *it's not because God changed the assignment.*

It's because something extra was added.

And anything added *that God did not assign* can be released.

Joy is waiting on the other side of that release.

Because ministry—
   is way too good not to enjoy it.

3

THE DAY MINISTRY BECAME HEAVY

Most leaders can remember the day ministry became heavy.

It wasn't announced.
It wasn't dramatic.
There was no obvious failure attached to it.

It was just... different.

You didn't stop *loving God.*
You didn't stop *believing the Word.*
You didn't stop *preaching, leading, serving, or showing up.*

But something shifted inside.

The joy didn't disappear overnight—*it thinned.*
The fire didn't go out—*it dimmed.*
The calling didn't leave—*it started to weigh more than it lifted.*

And if you're honest, you don't remember exactly when it happened—*only that one day you realized it had*.

THE MOMENT NO ONE PREPARES YOU FOR

No one prepares leaders for this moment.

They prepare you for *opposition*.
They prepare you for *sacrifice*.
They prepare you for *long hours and hard seasons*.

But no one tells you what to do when **ministry stops being exhilarating and starts being heavy**.

Because heaviness doesn't feel like failure.
It feels like responsibility.

And responsible leaders rarely complain about responsibility.

So, you keep going.

HOW HEAVINESS SNEAKS IN

Heaviness usually doesn't come from one big thing.

It comes from accumulation.

A hard season that *never fully resolved*.
A disappointment *you never grieved*.
A betrayal you *spiritualized instead of processed*.

A criticism that *lodged deeper than you admitted.*

You told yourself:

"I'm fine."
   "It's part of leadership."
      "I'll deal with it later."

But "later" never came.

And unprocessed weight *always settles somewhere.*

What you don't feel immediately, you carry eventually.

WHEN THE PULPIT COSTS MORE THAN IT GIVES

You remember when preaching energized you.

You studied the Word with anticipation.
You stepped into the pulpit with expectancy.
You left drained—but full.

Then something changed.

You still preach—*but it costs more.*
You still prepare—*but it feels heavier.*
You still deliver—*but you don't always recover the same way.*

The anointing is still there—**but the delight feels distant**.

And you don't know how to explain that without sounding ungrateful.

So, you don't.

THE UNPROCESSED GRIEF OF LEADERS

One of the most overlooked realities of ministry is grief.

Leaders grieve differently.

You grieve:

- People who left suddenly
- Leaders who disappointed you
- Seasons that didn't turn out the way you prayed
- Losses you had to absorb quietly

And often, you grieve alone.

Because who do leaders grieve with when *they're expected to be the strong ones*?

Grief that isn't acknowledged doesn't disappear.

It transforms into heaviness.

And heaviness, over time, *erodes joy.*

WHEN FAITHFULNESS BECOMES FUNCTIONAL

At some point, ministry can become *functional* instead of *joyful*.

You know how to do it.
You're good at it.
You've done it long enough to operate on instinct.

And functionality replaces fascination.

You still believe it's holy—*but it no longer feels alive in the same way.*

You *manage* moments instead of *marveling* at them.
You *execute* services instead of *encountering* God within them.

And when fascination fades, *joy follows.*

THE DANGEROUS THOUGHT LEADERS NEVER SAY OUT LOUD

Here's the thought leaders rarely admit—even to themselves:

"I don't know when this started feeling this heavy."

Because admitting heaviness *feels like weakness.*
Because leaders assume *heaviness means ingratitude.*
Because they confuse *weight with faithfulness.*

But heaviness is not proof of obedience.

It's proof something is being *carried without replenishment.*

DAVID KNEW THIS MOMENT

David knew this moment.

Psalm after psalm reveals it:
  "My soul is cast down within me."
    "My strength fails because of my affliction."
      "Restore to me the joy of Your salvation."

David didn't ask for a new calling.
He asked for restored joy.

Because joy can be lost even when obedience remains.

WHEN PRESENCE IS REPLACED
BY PERFORMANCE

This is where heaviness usually takes root.

Not when you stop praying—*but when prayer becomes preparation.*

Not when you stop worshiping—*but when worship becomes leadership.*

Not when you stop seeking God—*but when seeking God becomes task-oriented.*

Presence becomes *functional*.
Intimacy becomes *instrumental*.

And the soul feels the difference—**even if the schedule doesn't allow you to acknowledge it**.

Joy cannot survive long without presence.

THE MOMENT OF HONEST RECKONING

This chapter asks you to pause—*not rush*.

To sit with one question:

When did ministry start feeling heavy—and what happened around that time?

Not to blame.
Not to quit.
But to recognize.

Because recognition is the beginning of restoration.

God is not offended by your honesty.
He's inviting it.

HEAVINESS IS NOT THE END OF THE STORY

The day ministry became heavy was not the day your calling diminished.

It was the day something needed attention.

Joy didn't leave because God withdrew.
Joy thinned because weight accumulated.

And anything accumulated can be addressed.

The heaviness you feel is not a verdict.
It's a signal.

A signal calling you back—not to *less faithfulness*—
but to *deeper presence*.

Because ministry—
    is way too good not to enjoy it.

4

EXHAUSTION IS NOT A SPIRITUAL GIFT

Somewhere along the way, the church learned to applaud exhaustion.

We didn't mean to.
It didn't start maliciously.
It developed slowly—almost sincerely.

We began to celebrate leaders who never stopped.

Who were always available ... answered every call ... filled every gap ... carried every burden.

We called it *sacrifice*.
We called it *faithfulness*.
We called it *leadership*.

But Scripture never calls it holy.

Exhaustion is not a fruit of the Spirit.
Burnout is not a badge of honor.

Depletion is not proof of devotion.

And yet, many leaders quietly believe that being tired all the time is simply "the cost of the call."

It isn't.

HOW WE LEARNED TO SPIRITUALIZE FATIGUE

Most leaders never decide to glorify exhaustion.

They absorb it.

They watch admired leaders run themselves into the ground and hear people say, *"That's what real ministry looks like."*

They hear stories of sacrifice *without hearing stories of recovery.*

They internalize the idea that rest is optional—*but availability is mandatory.*

So, when fatigue shows up, instead of listening to it, they rebuke it.

Instead of tending to it, they *push through it.*
Instead of acknowledging it, they *spiritualize it.*

"This is just the season."
"This is the price of obedience."
"This is what leadership costs."

But God never asked leaders to pay for ministry with their health, their joy, or their soul.

ELIJAH: ANOINTED, VICTORIOUS, AND EXHAUSTED

Elijah had just experienced one of the greatest moments in biblical history.

Fire fell from heaven.
False prophets were defeated.
The nation saw the power of God.

And immediately afterward—**Elijah collapsed**.

Not into sin.
Not into doubt.

Into exhaustion.

He ran.
He hid.
He asked God to take his life.

And what did God do?

God did not rebuke him.
God did not correct his theology.
God did not tell him to pray harder.

God let him sleep ... fed him ... restored his strength.

Only after rest came revelation.

God treated Elijah's exhaustion as a human need—
not a spiritual failure.

If exhaustion were holiness, God would have praised Elijah for it.

Instead, He healed it.

WHY TIRED LEADERS MAKE DANGEROUS DECISIONS

Exhaustion clouds discernment.

When leaders are depleted:

- *Everything feels urgent*
- *Criticism feels personal*
- *Problems feel overwhelming*
- *Small issues feel catastrophic*

Exhausted leaders don't stop caring.
They stop processing clearly.

That's why Scripture so often connects strength with renewal.

Isaiah didn't say, *"Those who grind harder will renew their strength."*

He said, *"Those who wait upon the Lord."*

Waiting is not weakness.
It is wisdom.

JESUS RESTED — AND HE WAS SINLESS

Jesus withdrew often.

From *crowds*.
From *demand*.
From *expectation*.

He rested before choosing the disciples.
He slept during the storm.
He withdrew after miracles.

If rest were laziness, Jesus would never have practiced it.

And if rest were optional, *Jesus would never have modeled it.*

Jesus understood something leaders often forget:

You cannot continually pour out what you never replenish.

THE DANGEROUS CONFUSION BETWEEN SACRIFICE AND SELF-HARM

Sacrifice is *obedience*.
Self-destruction is *imbalance*.

Sacrifice has purpose.
Self-destruction has no end.

God honors sacrifice.
God rescues from self-destruction.

Many leaders crossed the line without noticing.

They didn't choose burnout.
They *drifted into it*—one yes at a time.

Joy didn't disappear because they stopped loving God.

Joy disappeared because *exhaustion muted their soul.*

WHY JOY IS OFTEN THE FIRST CASUALTY

Joy requires margin.

Margin to *breathe.*
Margin to *feel.*
Margin to *delight.*

Exhaustion consumes margin.

When leaders are exhausted:

- Joy feels irresponsible
- Rest feels selfish
- Laughter feels inappropriate

So joy gets postponed ... and postponed joy eventually disappears.

But joy is not a luxury.

It is strength.

And leaders without joy eventually lead tired cultures.

THE GENTLE INVITATION GOD MAKES TO TIRED LEADERS

Jesus didn't say, "Come to Me when you've proven your endurance."

He said, "Come to Me, all who are weary and heavy-laden."

Weary leaders are not *weak leaders*.
They are *human leaders*.

And God is not disappointed by your exhaustion.
He is *inviting you to bring it to Him*.

THE QUESTION THIS CHAPTER ASKS YOU

Let this question linger:

What exhaustion have I been calling obedience?

Where have I ignored the limits God designed? *Where have I postponed rest in the name of responsibility?* Where has joy thinned because fatigue went unaddressed?

This is not an accusation. *It is an invitation.*

God never intended ministry to drain the life out of you.

He intended it to flow through you.

A WORD OF HOPE BEFORE YOU TURN THE PAGE

Exhaustion does not disqualify you.

It reveals a need.

And needs, when acknowledged, become *doorways for grace.*

Joy can return.
Strength can be renewed.
Delight can be restored.

Because ministry—
        is way too good not to enjoy it.

5

THE JOY OF THE LORD IS YOUR STRENGTH

Nehemiah did not say this to people living in comfort.

He said it to people standing in ruins.

The walls of Jerusalem *were broken.*
Homes *were unfinished.*
The work *was overwhelming.*
The people *were tired.*

And yet, in the middle of rubble and rebuilding, Nehemiah stood and declared something that sounds almost irresponsible to weary ears:

"The joy of the Lord is your strength."

Not strategy.
Not stamina.
Not sheer willpower.

Joy.

Which means joy is not the *result of strength*.
Joy is the *source of it*.

JOY IS NOT A REWARD FOR EASY SEASONS

Many leaders assume joy comes *after* the pressure lifts.

After the season changes.
After the crisis passes.
After the workload lightens.

But Nehemiah didn't wait for the walls to be finished before he talked about joy.

He understood something essential:

Joy is not a **luxury reserved for light seasons**.
Joy is a ***necessity for heavy ones***.

Without joy, *strength erodes*.
Without joy, *perseverance becomes punishment*.
Without joy, *obedience becomes hollow*.

Joy is not denial of difficulty. **Joy is defiance of despair.**

WHAT JOY IS — AND WHAT IT IS NOT

Joy is not happiness.

Happiness responds to circumstances.

Joy flows from connection.

Joy is not optimism.

Optimism believes things will improve.
Joy believes God is present now.

Joy is not personality-based.

Some leaders are naturally expressive.
Others are reflective and reserved.

Joy is not volume—it is vitality.

Joy is not pretending everything is fine.
Joy is knowing God is faithful even when things are hard.

Joy is not fragile.

It is resilient.

WHY NEHEMIAH CONNECTED JOY TO STRENGTH

Strength without joy becomes *endurance.*
Endurance without joy becomes *survival.*
Survival without joy becomes *resentment.*

Nehemiah knew something leaders often learn late:

You cannot lead long without joy.

Joy does not make leadership *easier.*

It makes leadership *sustainable*.

Joy fuels vision.
Joy softens sacrifice.
Joy anchors obedience when results lag behind effort.

Without joy, leaders may last—**but they won't thrive**.

THE JOY OF THE LORD — NOT THE JOY OF RESULTS

Notice the phrase carefully:

"The joy of the Lord."

Not the *joy of success*.
Not the *joy of growth*.
Not the *joy of affirmation*.

The joy of the Lord.

Joy *rooted in outcomes* will always be fragile.
Joy *rooted in God* is durable.

If your joy depends on attendance, *it will fluctuate*.
If your joy depends on feedback, *it will shrink*.
If your joy depends on momentum, *it will disappear* in slow seasons.

But when joy flows from the Lord Himself, it is not threatened by setbacks.

This is why leaders can be *faithful in obscurity*.
This is why missionaries *endure unseen labor*.
This is why pastors keep *preaching in small rooms*
with big faith.

Their joy is not circumstantial—**it is relational**.

WHY JOY DISAPPEARS EVEN WHEN GOD DOESN'T

Joy disappears not because God withdraws—but
because leaders *drift from connection to completion*.

We focus on:

- *Finishing the sermon*
- *Solving the problem*
- *Leading the meeting*
- *Managing the outcome*

And slowly, God becomes the *means* instead of the
delight.

Joy is lost not when leaders *stop believing*—but
when they *stop abiding*.

**Jesus said, "These things I have spoken to
you, that My joy may remain in you."**

Remain.
Stay.
Abide.

Joy does not come from *visiting God occasionally*.

Joy comes from *remaining with Him consistently*.

THE STRENGTH JOY PROVIDES
THAT NOTHING ELSE CAN

Joy gives strength in ways discipline cannot.

Joy allows leaders to:

- Stay soft without becoming sentimental
- Stay faithful without becoming rigid
- Stay hopeful without becoming naive

Joy keeps leaders human.

When joy is present:

- Correction is gentle
- Vision is hopeful
- Sacrifice feels meaningful

When joy is absent:

- Leadership becomes harsh
- Vision narrows
- Sacrifice feels transactional

Joy protects the soul of the leader.

WHY SOME STRONG LEADERS
ARE ACTUALLY WEAK

Some leaders appear strong—but are *inwardly exhausted*.

They have grit—*but not gladness.*
They have discipline—*but not delight.*
They have resolve—*but not rest.*

And eventually, grit without joy breaks.

Joy is not weakness.
Joy is reinforcement.

Nehemiah didn't tell the people to push harder.
He told them to celebrate, to eat, to drink, to rejoice.

Why?

Because joy rebuilds what fatigue destroys.

THE INVITATION TO RECLAIM JOY

Joy does not return through *effort.*
It returns through *attention.*

Attention to:

- Presence
- *Gratitude*
- Wonder
- *Communion*

Joy returns when leaders stop asking:

"How am I doing?"

And start asking,

"Where is God meeting me right now?"

Joy grows where God is noticed.

A QUIET MOMENT BEFORE MOVING ON

Sit with this truth:

If joy is your strength, then joylessness is not harmless.

It doesn't just affect your mood.

It affects your endurance.
Your discernment.
Your longevity.

This chapter is not calling you to *hype*.
It's calling you to **reconnection**.

Because joy does not have to be *chased*.
It has to be **received**.

THE PROMISE THIS CHAPTER LEAVES YOU WITH

Joy is not gone forever.
It has not expired.
It has not disqualified you.

Joy is waiting in the presence of the Lord.

And when joy returns, strength follows.

Because ministry—
is way too good not to enjoy it.

— 6 —

JESUS NEVER ASKED YOU TO DIE WITHOUT RESURRECTION

There is a sentence many leaders believe but rarely say out loud:

"This is just how ministry is supposed to feel."

Heavy.
　　Costly.
　　　　Draining.
　　　　　　Life-consuming.

And when leaders feel that way long enough, they spiritualize it. **They quote verses about dying to self.** They talk about sacrifice. **They normalize depletion.**

But here is a truth that must be said plainly:

Jesus never asked you to die without resurrection.

THE DANGEROUS MISUSE OF
"DYING TO SELF"

Jesus did call us to *deny ourselves.*
He did call us to *take up our cross.*
He did call us to *lay down our lives.*

But He never called us to remain buried.

Self-denial is not self-erasure.

The cross was never meant to be a permanent residence.

Resurrection was always part of the story.

Somewhere along the way, many leaders learned how to die—*but never learned how to live again.*

They learned how to *sacrifice.*
They learned how to *endure.*
They learned how to *pour out.*

But they were never taught how to receive.

And when resurrection is removed from the equation, death becomes *destructive* instead of *redemptive.*

WHY LEADERS STAY IN
PERPETUAL GOOD FRIDAY

Good Friday is holy—*but it is not the end.*

Yet many leaders live their entire ministry lives in perpetual crucifixion.

They preach *resurrection*.
They believe *resurrection*.
But they don't *experience resurrection*.

They live in constant loss:

- Loss of energy
- Loss of delight
- Loss of margin
- Loss of joy

And they call it faithfulness.

But Jesus never stayed on the cross.
And He never asked you to either.

PAUL UNDERSTOOD THE RHYTHM OF DEATH AND LIFE

Paul wrote about dying daily—but he also wrote about being renewed daily.

Outwardly wasting.
Inwardly renewed.

Death and life.
Surrender and strengthening.
Sacrifice and joy.

Paul did not preach a gospel of slow spiritual erosion.

He preached a gospel of **continual renewal**.

If your ministry only knows death and never knows renewal, something has been misunderstood.

WHY SOME LEADERS FEAR RESURRECTION

This may be uncomfortable—*but it needs to be said.*

Some leaders fear resurrection because resurrection requires:

- Letting go
- *Rest*
- Receiving
- *Relearning joy*

And joy can feel dangerous to wounded leaders.

Joy feels *vulnerable.*
Joy feels *exposed.*
Joy feels like something that *could be taken away again.*

So leaders settle for survival.
They learn how to function without feeling.
They stay faithful—but guarded.

But guarded leaders cannot fully experience resurrection.

RESURRECTION IS NOT SELFISH — IT IS NECESSARY

Some leaders equate resurrection with indulgence.

They worry:

"If I enjoy ministry again, will I lose my edge?"
"If I rest, will I become lazy?"
"If I feel joy, will I become complacent?"

But resurrection does not dull obedience.

It revitalizes it.

Jesus rose with scars—but *also with strength.*
Resurrection did not erase the cost.

It redeemed it.

And when leaders experience resurrection:

- Compassion deepens
- *Perspective widens*
- Ministry becomes sustainable

Resurrection does not make you careless.
It makes you alive.

WHY JOY IS OFTEN POSTPONED IN MINISTRY

Many leaders believe joy must wait.

After the season ends.
After the problem resolves.
After the church stabilizes.
After the breakthrough comes.

But resurrection was not delayed until conditions were perfect.

It came while the scars were still visible.

Joy does not require a pain-free life.
It requires a living Savior.

THE INVITATION JESUS KEEPS MAKING

Jesus' invitation was never just *"Follow Me."*
It was also *"Come to Me."*

Come when weary.
Come when heavy.
Come when spent.

Jesus never admired exhaustion.
He relieved it.

And He never glorified joylessness.
He restored joy.

A HOLY CONFRONTATION WITH A FALSE BELIEF

Let this question search you:

Have I confused ongoing depletion with faithfulness?

Where have I accepted death without expecting resurrection?
Where have I poured out without receiving?
Where have I stayed buried when Jesus was calling me to rise?

This is not an accusation.
It is a correction.

And correction is grace.

THE PROMISE OF THIS CHAPTER

Resurrection is not just theological.
It is experiential.

Jesus still restores.
Still renews.
Still revives.

You do not have to choose between sacrifice and joy.
You were never meant to.

Because ministry was never designed to kill you.

It was designed to carry life.

And life—
is way too good not to enjoy it.

THE DIFFERENCE BETWEEN SACRIFICE AND SELF-DESTRUCTION

Most leaders never intend to harm themselves.

They intend to serve.
They intend to obey.
They intend to be faithful.

Self-destruction is rarely a conscious choice in ministry.

It is usually the *unintended consequence* of *misunderstood sacrifice.*

Sacrifice and self-destruction look similar on the surface.

Both involve giving.
Both involve cost.
Both involve saying yes when it would be easier to say no.

But only one of them is holy.

WHAT SACRIFICE IS — AND WHAT IT IS NOT

Sacrifice is *intentional.*
Self-destruction is *cumulative.*

Sacrifice is *offered freely.*
Self-destruction is often *fueled by fear.*

Sacrifice has *boundaries.*
Self-destruction *ignores them.*

God honors sacrifice because it flows from obedience.

God intervenes in self-destruction because it flows from imbalance.

The tragedy is that many leaders crossed the line slowly—*so slowly they didn't notice.*

What started as obedience turned into overextension. *What started as availability turned into depletion.* What started as love turned into obligation.

And joy quietly disappeared along the way.

WHY LEADERS STRUGGLE TO SEE THE LINE

Leaders struggle to see the difference because

ministry *rewards sacrifice publicly*—but rarely *addresses sustainability privately*.

People applaud when you *give more*.
People celebrate when you *stay longer*.
People assume capacity because they *see consistency*.

And leaders internalize this message:

"If I can do it, *I should*."
   "If I don't do it, *I'm failing*."
      "If I stop, *I'm selfish*."

But ability is not always assignment.

Just because you *can* carry something doesn't mean God asked you to.

JESUS MODELED SACRIFICE — NEVER SELF-DESTRUCTION

Jesus gave everything—***but He did not destroy Himself***.

He laid down His life at the appointed time—*not prematurely*.
He poured Himself out—*but withdrew regularly*.
He loved deeply—*but honored limits*.

Jesus never healed everyone.
Never met every demand.
Never answered every expectation.

And yet—*He fulfilled His mission completely.*

Jesus did not measure faithfulness by exhaustion but *by obedience*.

HOW SELF-DESTRUCTION HIDES IN GOOD INTENTIONS

Self-destruction often disguises itself as:

- Being indispensable
- *Being endlessly available*
- Being unwilling to disappoint
- *Being afraid to delegate*

It whispers:

"If I rest, things will fall apart."
"If I slow down, I'll lose momentum."
"If I say no, I'll lose trust."

But those whispers are not the voice of God.
They are the voice of fear.

Fear always demands more than grace supplies.

THE ROLE OF GUILT IN SELF-DESTRUCTIVE MINISTRY

Guilt is a powerful motivator—*and a poor master.*

Many leaders operate under quiet guilt:

Guilt for resting ... for enjoying ministry ...

for protecting time ... for not doing more.

But guilt-driven ministry is *unsustainable*.

God leads through calling—*not coercion*.
Grace—*not guilt*.

When guilt drives sacrifice, **self-destruction is never far behind**.

WHY JOY DISAPPEARS FIRST

Joy cannot survive in *self-destructive systems*.

When leaders constantly override limits:

- Joy feels irresponsible
- *Rest feels disobedient*
- Delight feels undeserved

So, joy is *postponed*.
Then *ignored*.
Then *forgotten*.

And eventually, leaders *forget they were ever allowed to enjoy the call*.

But God never revoked that permission.

A NECESSARY MOMENT OF DISCERNMENT

This chapter asks you to slow down and discern—*not judge*.

Ask yourself: *What sacrifices am I making that God is actually asking of me?*

And then ask: *What sacrifices am I making out of fear, guilt, or pressure?*

One leads to life. *The other leads to erosion.*

And the difference matters.

REDEFINING FAITHFULNESS

Faithfulness is not *doing everything*.
It is doing **what God assigned**.

Faithfulness is not *limitless availability*.
It is **obedient stewardship**.

Faithfulness is not *being indispensable*.
It is being **dependent on God**.

When faithfulness is rightly defined, **joy finds room to return**.

THE FREEDOM ON THE OTHER SIDE OF THIS LINE

When leaders reclaim this distinction:

- Rest becomes *permissible*
- Joy becomes **appropriate**
- Boundaries become *holy*
- Ministry becomes **sustainable**

You don't become less committed.
You become more aligned.

And alignment always brings relief.

THE PROMISE THIS CHAPTER
LEAVES YOU WITH

God never asked you to destroy yourself to serve
Him.

He asked you to *follow Him*—and following Jesus
always leads to life.

Sacrifice is still holy.
But self-destruction is not.

And when that line is reclaimed, *joy has space to
breathe again*.

Because ministry—
    is way **TOO GOOD** not to enjoy it.

— 8 —

WHY GOD CARES HOW YOU FEEL ABOUT YOUR CALLING

Many leaders believe God cares *that* they serve—but not *how* they feel while serving.

They assume obedience is all that matters.

Attitude feels *secondary*.
Emotion feels *irrelevant*.

So when joy fades, they don't bring it to God. *They push past it.*

They suppress it.

They assume feeling weary or empty is simply **part of the cost**.

But Scripture tells a different story.

God has always cared about the inner life of His servants—**not just their outward obedience**.

OBEDIENCE WITHOUT DELIGHT
WAS NEVER GOD'S DESIGN

From the beginning, God didn't just want compliance—*He wanted communion.*

He didn't merely command Israel to serve Him. He invited them to *delight* in Him.

"Serve the Lord with gladness."
"Delight yourself in the Lord."
"Rejoice in the Lord always."

These are not emotional suggestions.
They are spiritual indicators.

God never separated *obedience* from *affection.*

We did.

WHY LEADERS LEARN TO
DISCONNECT FROM THEIR
EMOTIONS

Leadership trains people to override feelings.

You lead *when tired.*
You show up *when discouraged.*
You minister *when hurting.*

And over time, you learn to **function without feeling**.

That skill helps you survive emergencies—but it can

quietly *numb your soul.*

Eventually, leaders stop asking: *"How am I doing inside?"*

They replace it with: *"What needs to be done?"*

But ignoring the inner life **doesn't make it disappear**.

It simply **pushes it underground**—*where it eventually shapes everything.*

THE MYTH THAT EMOTIONS ARE UNTRUSTWORTHY

Some leaders were taught that emotions are unreliable, even dangerous.

So they learned to *distrust joy.*
To **minimize sorrow**.
To *compartmentalize fear*.
To **ignore fatigue**.

But Scripture never treats emotions as enemies.
It treats them as signals.

The Psalms are filled with emotion.
Jesus Himself **wept, rejoiced, groaned, and grieved**.

God is not threatened by how you feel.
He invites you to bring it to Him.

WHY GOD ADDRESSES THE
HEART BEFORE THE TASK

Throughout Scripture, God often addresses how His servants feel *before addressing what they do*.

To Joshua, He said, **"Do not be afraid."**
To Elijah, He provided *rest before instruction*.
To David, He *restored joy before restoring leadership*.

Why?

Because God knows leaders do not lead from tasks. *They lead from the heart*.

When the heart is depleted, **ministry becomes hollow**.

When the heart is alive, **ministry flows naturally**.

THE COST OF IGNORING HOW
YOU FEEL

Ignoring your emotional life does not make you more spiritual.

It makes you disconnected.

Disconnected leaders:

- *React* instead of *respond*
- *Protect* themselves instead of *pastoring*
- Lead with *control* instead of *compassion*

Joy fades not because leaders are weak—but *because they stop tending the inner life.*

God cares how you feel because your feelings shape how you serve.

WHEN JOY FEELS INAPPROPRIATE

Some leaders feel guilty enjoying ministry.

They *see pain.*
They *carry burdens.*
They *feel the weight of brokenness.*

So, joy feels inappropriate—almost disrespectful.

But joy is not a denial of pain.
It is a declaration that pain does not have the final word.

God is not honored by joyless servants.

He is honored by servants who trust Him enough to rejoice even in difficulty.

GOD'S INVITATION IS NOT JUST "SERVE ME" — IT IS "WALK WITH ME"

Walking implies *relationship.*
Relationship includes **emotion.**
Emotion requires *honesty.*

God does not want a servant who **performs without feeling**. *He wants a son or daughter who serves from connection*.

Joy flows naturally from connection.
When connection fades, joy follows.

A HOLY QUESTION FOR SELF-EXAMINATION

Pause here and ask:

When was the last time I told God how ministry actually feels?

Not how it looks.
　　Not how it's supposed to feel.
　　　　But how it really feels.

God is not waiting for you to fix it.

He's waiting for you to share it.

THE PROMISE OF THIS CHAPTER

God cares how you feel—not because feelings define truth, *but because they reveal where truth has drifted from intimacy.*

Joy is not an **add-on to calling**. It is a **byproduct of relationship**.

And relationship is always God's priority.

Because ministry—
   is WAY too GOOD *not to enjoy it.*

9

THE TYRANNY OF EXPECTATIONS

Expectations rarely introduce themselves as enemies.

They come dressed as responsibility.
They sound like commitment.
They feel like faithfulness.

But over time, expectations—especially unspoken ones—can become one of the **heaviest burdens a leader carries**.

And joy is often their first casualty.

EXPECTATIONS ARE HEAVY BECAUSE THEY ARE INVISIBLE

Most leaders can identify *workloads*.
They can name *schedules*.
They can list *responsibilities*.

But expectations are harder to see.

They linger in the background.

- Expectations from people who never say them out loud
- *Expectations from systems that reward performance over health*
- Expectations from cultures that equate busyness with faithfulness
- *Expectations leaders place on themselves in the name of excellence*

Because expectations are often unnamed, they become unchecked.

And unchecked expectations quietly rule the soul.

THE EXPECTATION TO ALWAYS BE AVAILABLE

Many leaders live under the unspoken rule:

"You should always be reachable."

If you're unavailable, you *feel guilty*.
If you miss a call, you **replay it**.
If you say no, you *explain yourself*.

Availability becomes the *measure of love*.
Responsiveness becomes the *proof of faithfulness*.

But Jesus was not always available.

He *withdrew*.
He **rested**.
He walked away from crowds *still needing healing*.

And no one accused Him of being unfaithful.

Jesus did not meet every expectation placed upon Him.
He met every expectation placed by the Father.

There is a difference.

WHEN EXPECTATIONS REPLACE CALLING

Calling is *clarifying*.
Expectations are *confusing*.

Calling says: *"This is what God asked of you."*

Expectations say: *"This is what everyone wants from you."*

When expectations replace calling:

- Leaders become *reactive* instead of *intentional*
- Boundaries feel *selfish*
- Joy feels *irresponsible*

You wake up responding instead of leading.
You carry guilt instead of grace.
You feel pressure instead of purpose.

And joy slowly suffocates under the weight of pleasing everyone.

THE IMPOSSIBLE TASK OF MEETING EVERY EXPECTATION

Here is a hard truth leaders must accept:

You cannot meet every expectation—and trying to will cost you your joy.

Some expectations contradict each other.
Some expectations change constantly.
Some expectations are unreasonable.
Some expectations were never meant to be met.

Trying to meet them all will exhaust you—and still leave people disappointed.

Jesus disappointed people.
Paul disappointed churches.
Moses disappointed Israel.

Faithfulness does not eliminate disappointment. *It clarifies allegiance.*

THE EXPECTATIONS LEADERS PLACE ON THEMSELVES

Some of the heaviest expectations don't come from others.

They come from within.

Leaders expect themselves to:

- Always be strong
- *Always have answers*
- Always handle criticism well
- *Always be emotionally available*

These self-imposed expectations **feel noble**.
But they quietly **deny humanity**.

God never asked you to be *omnipresent, omniscient,*
or *invulnerable.*

Those are **divine attributes**—not **leadership
requirements**.

HOW EXPECTATIONS DRAIN JOY

Expectations drain joy because they create constant
evaluation.

You begin asking:
"Did I do enough?"
  "Did I handle that right?"
    "Did I disappoint someone?"

Instead of:
"Was I obedient?"
  "Was I present with God?"
    "Was I faithful to my assignment?"

Evaluation replaces gratitude.
Pressure replaces peace.
And joy fades.

JESUS AND THE FREEDOM FROM EXPECTATIONS

Jesus lived with clarity.

He knew who He was.
He knew why He was sent.
He knew what belonged to Him—and what didn't.

When expectations conflicted with calling, **He chose calling every time**.

That clarity gave Him freedom.
That freedom protected His joy.

Leaders lose joy not because they care too much— but because they care about too many voices.

THE HOLY PRACTICE OF DISAPPOINTING PEOPLE

This may be one of the most freeing truths a leader ever learns:

Disappointing people is sometimes a sign of obedience.

When you choose *presence* over *performance*.
When you choose *rest* over *responsiveness*.
When you choose *calling* over *approval*.

Disappointment is **not failure**.
It is often the **byproduct of faithfulness**.

And joy returns when approval is relocated—*from people to God.*

A MOMENT OF HONEST ASSESSMENT

Pause and ask yourself:

Whose expectations am I currently carrying that God never assigned?

Where have I confused *faithfulness* with *people-pleasing*?

What expectation, if released, ***would immediately lighten my soul?***

Joy often returns not when workload changes—but when *expectations are redefined.*

THE PROMISE OF THIS CHAPTER

You were never meant to *live under the tyranny of expectations.*

You were called to **live under the guidance of the Spirit**.

When expectations lose their grip, *joy finds room again.*

Because leadership was never meant to feel like a constant performance review.

It was meant to be a walk with God.

And ministry—
    is way

        TOO GOOD

           not to enjoy it!

10

WHEN METRICS REPLACE MIRACLES

Most leaders don't start ministry obsessed with numbers.

They start with a call ... *a burden* ... a moment with God they cannot escape.

They don't count conversions at first—*they celebrate them.*
They don't track attendance at first—**they marvel at faces**.
They don't analyze engagement—*they rejoice over transformation.*

But somewhere along the journey, **numbers begin to speak louder than stories**.

And when metrics replace miracles, *joy quietly slips away*.

WHEN NUMBERS STOP BEING TOOLS AND START BECOMING VOICES

Metrics are not evil.

They can help leaders steward resources.
They can reveal trends.
They can inform decisions.

But metrics were never meant to become measures of worth.

The danger comes when numbers *stop being tools* and *start being voices*.

Voices that say:

"You're growing—*or you're failing.*"
"You're effective—*or you're irrelevant.*"
"You're winning—*or you're falling behind.*"

And suddenly, leaders start **listening to spreadsheets more than the Spirit**.

THE SUBTLE SHIFT FROM FAITHFULNESS TO PERFORMANCE

The shift happens quietly.

You still pray—but you also *check the numbers*.
You still preach—but you *measure response*.

You still serve—but you *assess impact constantly*.

Faithfulness becomes *filtered through performance*.
Obedience becomes *evaluated by outcomes*.

And when outcomes fluctuate—*as they always do*—
joy fluctuates with them.

Joy tied to metrics is fragile.
It *rises* and *falls* with attendance, giving,
engagement, and visibility.

But joy tied to obedience is resilient.

WHY METRICS DRAIN JOY EVEN WHEN THEY IMPROVE

Ironically, metrics don't just drain joy when they're
bad.

They drain joy even when they're good.

Because success *raises expectations*.
Momentum **creates pressure**.
Growth *introduces comparison*.

You celebrate briefly—**then brace yourself to
sustain it**.

Joy doesn't last long when success becomes
something you must *maintain* rather than *receive*.

THE BIBLICAL WARNING
AGAINST COUNTING

David once counted Israel—not because God asked him to, but because *he wanted reassurance*.

And Scripture records it as sin—not because numbers were counted, but ***because trust shifted***.

Counting became a *substitute for confidence in God*.

Leaders don't drift when they track information. They drift when they *seek identity in it*.

WHAT JESUS COUNTED — AND
WHAT HE DIDN'T

Jesus rarely counted crowds.
He noticed individuals.

He saw Zacchaeus *in a tree*.
He noticed a woman *at a well*.
He honored a *widow's mite*.
He celebrated *one lost sheep*.

Jesus was not impressed by size.
He was moved by faith.

And His joy flowed from obedience to the Father—*not from visible results*.

WHEN COMPARISON ENTERS THE ROOM

Metrics invite comparison.

Who's growing faster.
Who's reaching more.
Who's doing better with less.

Comparison is subtle—**but deadly to joy**.

It convinces leaders they are behind *when God may simply be leading them differently.*

Comparison steals **contentment**.
Contentment fuels *joy*.

THE WEIGHT OF INVISIBLE FAITHFULNESS

Some of the most faithful ministry happens where metrics are unimpressive.

In small rooms.
In slow seasons.
In unseen places.

Counseling no one applauds.
Prayers no one hears.
Faithfulness no one counts.

And if joy depends on visible success, leaders in these places *will feel invisible.*

But heaven never overlooks unseen obedience.

God counts faithfulness differently.

REDEFINING SUCCESS THROUGH GOD'S EYES

Success in Scripture is rarely measured by size.

It is measured by *obedience ... trust ... endurance.*

By love.

Many leaders are far more successful than they feel—because they're *measuring with the wrong ruler.*

Joy returns when leaders redefine success the way God does.

A NECESSARY QUESTION FOR MODERN LEADERS

Pause and ask:

What numbers have been speaking too loudly in my soul?

Where have I allowed metrics to define my mood, my confidence, or my joy?

What miracle might I be overlooking because I'm focused on measurement instead of meaning?

Joy often returns when leaders **stop counting what God never asked them to count**.

THE PROMISE OF THIS CHAPTER

Metrics can inform leadership—but they should never define it.

Miracles still matter.
Stories still matter.
People still matter.

And obedience—quiet, faithful obedience— still delights God.

When metrics are put back in their place, joy can breathe again.

Because ministry—
is way too good
not to enjoy it.

11

FAMILIARITY WITH THE HOLY

There is a danger that comes not from distance—**but from closeness**.

It does not threaten outsiders.
It quietly affects insiders.

It does not target skeptics.
It slowly dulls servants.

It is the danger of becoming too familiar with the holy.

And when familiarity sets in, *joy is often the first thing lost*.

WHEN HOLY THINGS BECOME ROUTINE

Leaders handle holy things every day.

Scripture.
   Prayer.
      Worship.
         Sacred moments.
            Life-changing conversations.

And over time, what was **once wondrous can become routine**.

Not because leaders **stop believing**.
But because repetition *dulls awareness*.

You still believe the Word is powerful.
You just don't feel its weight the same way.
You still know worship is sacred.
You just lead it more than you enter it.

And when wonder fades, joy follows.

THE PRIESTS WHO HANDLED HOLY THINGS DAILY

In the Old Testament, priests worked around holy things constantly.

The altar.
The sacrifices.
The presence of God.

But Scripture also warns us that familiarity can *breed irreverence*.

What was meant to inspire awe can become mechanical.

What was meant to stir joy can become routine.

You can work around God and **_forget to stand in awe of Him_**.

WHY FAMILIARITY DULLS JOY

Joy thrives on *wonder*.
Wonder thrives on *awareness*.

Familiarity reduces awareness.

Leaders begin to *anticipate* moments instead of *encountering* them.

They *predict* responses instead of being *surprised*.

They *manage* holy moments instead of *marveling* at them.

Joy fades when surprise disappears.

WHEN WORSHIP BECOMES A ROLE

One of the most dangerous moments in leadership is when worship **_becomes a role rather than a response_**.

You know the songs.
You know the transitions.
You know the flow.

But your heart is *coordinating* rather than

communing.

And while the room may be filled with worship, ***the leader's soul can feel empty***.

Joy returns when worship stops being *something you lead* and becomes *something you enter again*.

THE SUBTLE LOSS OF REVERENCE

Reverence is not fear.
It is awareness.

Awareness that:

God is **present**.
God is *powerful*.
God is **holy**.

When reverence fades, *ministry becomes transactional*. When reverence fades, *joy becomes thin*.

Reverence reminds us that ***what we do matters because God is involved***.

JESUS AND THE WONDER OF THE KINGDOM

Jesus never lost wonder.

He **marveled at faith**.
He *rejoiced in the Spirit*.

He **gave thanks repeatedly**.

Though He knew the Father intimately, He never treated the holy as common.

And joy flowed freely from that reverence.

Closeness did not breed contempt.

It deepened delight.

WHY LEADERS STOP NOTICING MIRACLES

Miracles don't stop happening.
Leaders stop noticing them.

Answered prayers *become expected*.
Changed lives **become routine**.
Transformation becomes *part of the job description*.

But heaven never treats transformation casually.

What is common to us is *still celebrated in heaven*.

Joy returns when **leaders see familiar miracles with fresh eyes**.

RECLAIMING WONDER IS A CHOICE

Wonder does not return accidentally.
It returns intentionally.

Leaders must **choose to slow down**.

To notice.

To name the sacred.

To say again, *"This is holy ground."*

Joy grows where wonder is cultivated.

A MOMENT OF HOLY SELF-EXAMINATION

Pause and ask:

Where have I become overly familiar with holy things?

What sacred moments have I rushed through?

When was the last time ministry genuinely amazed me?

God has not stopped moving.
But familiarity may have muted your awareness.

THE PROMISE OF THIS CHAPTER

Wonder can be reclaimed.
Reverence can be restored.
Joy can return.

God is still holy.
Ministry is still sacred.

And what you are doing still matters.

Because ministry—

is *way* too good

not to *enjoy* it.

12

MINISTRY WITHOUT PRESENCE

It is possible to do ministry without presence.

Not without God's existence—
but without awareness of Him.

Not without *prayer—*
but without *intimacy.*

Not without **Scripture—**
but without **encounter.**

And when ministry continues without presence, *joy cannot survive for long.*

HOW PRESENCE SLOWLY BECOMES OPTIONAL

Ministry rarely abandons presence intentionally.

It replaces it subtly.

Prayer becomes **preparation**.
Worship becomes **leadership**.
Scripture becomes **content**.
Silence becomes **inefficient**.

You still pray—*but to get through the agenda*.
You still worship—**but with one eye on the clock**.
You still read Scripture—*but looking for material, not manna*.

And because the work still "works," the loss of presence goes unnoticed.

But your soul notices.

THE DIFFERENCE BETWEEN GOD'S POWER AND GOD'S PRESENCE

God's power can still operate when presence is neglected—*for a time*.

Samson discovered this tragically.
He shook himself, *expecting power*, unaware that **presence had departed**.

Leaders can still function.
Still preach.
Still lead.
Still see results.

But power without presence eventually becomes empty performance.

Presence is where joy lives.

Power without presence can *impress people*—but it cannot *sustain the soul.*

WHY BUSY LEADERS LOSE AWARENESS OF GOD

Busyness is not sin—*but it is dangerous.*

It fills space.
It consumes attention.
It crowds out stillness.

And **stillness** is where **presence** becomes **perceptible**.

Leaders often confuse God's patience with His permission.

They assume: *"If God were concerned, things wouldn't be working."*

But God is gracious. He allows *seasons of fruit* even while *inviting deeper intimacy.*

Joy fades not because God withdraws—***but because leaders stop noticing Him***.

WHEN GOD BECOMES A MEANS INSTEAD OF THE DELIGHT

One of the most painful shifts in ministry happens when God becomes ***the means*** to accomplish ministry instead of **the reason** for it.

You pray to preach well.
You worship to lead effectively.
You seek insight to solve problems.

God becomes useful—**but not enjoyed**.

And when God is no longer enjoyed, *joy evaporates.*

Joy is not the reward of ministry.
It is the fruit of presence.

MOSES KNEW WHAT PRESENCE MEANT

Moses said something stunning to God:

"If Your presence does not go with us, do not send us up from here."

He didn't say:

"If we don't have provision ... or protection ... or success."

Presence mattered more than progress.

Moses understood something many leaders forget:

You can reach the destination and still lose the delight if presence is absent.

WHY LEADERS FEEL EMPTY EVEN WHEN THEY'RE EFFECTIVE

This is one of the most confusing experiences for leaders.

Things are *working*.
People are *growing*.
The ministry is *active*.

And yet—**you feel empty**.

Because effectiveness can continue without intimacy—but **joy cannot**.

Joy requires *nearness*.
Joy requires *awareness*.
Joy requires *presence*.

And presence **cannot be rushed.**

THE COST OF LEADING WITHOUT PRESENCE

When leaders lead without presence:

- Compassion thins
- *Patience shortens*
- Discernment dulls
- *Cynicism creeps in*

Leadership becomes *mechanical*.
People become *projects*.

Ministry becomes *transactional*.

Not because leaders don't care—but because *presence has been sidelined*.

THE INVITATION BACK TO PRESENCE

God's invitation is not: *"Do more for Me."*

It is: *"Come be with Me."*

Presence is not reclaimed through **strategy**.
It is reclaimed through **stillness**.

Through:

- Unhurried prayer
- *Scripture without agenda*
- Worship without leadership
- *Silence without guilt*

Presence returns when **leaders give God their attention again**.

A QUIET BUT SEARCHING QUESTION

Pause and ask yourself:

When was the last time I was with God without trying to get something from Him?

Not insight.

Not answers.
Not solutions.

Just presence.

Joy often returns where presence is rediscovered.

THE PROMISE OF THIS CHAPTER

God has not moved.
God has not withdrawn.
God has not grown distant.

Presence is still available.
Still near.
Still inviting.

And when presence returns, *joy follows*.

Because ministry—
is **way too good** not **to enjoy it**.

13

RETURNING TO THE PRESENCE

Returning to the presence of God is rarely dramatic.

It is not usually *marked by fireworks*.
It does not always come with *immediate emotion*.
It often begins *quietly—**with awareness***.

Awareness that *something sacred has been missing*.
Awareness that *productivity replaced proximity*.
Awareness that you've been *doing God's work without lingering with God Himself*.

And that awareness *is not condemnation*.
It is invitation.

WHY RETURNING IS HARDER THAN LEAVING

Leaving the presence of God often happens **unintentionally**.
Returning requires **intention**.

Leaving happens through **distraction**.
Returning requires **attention**.

Leaving happens through **busyness**.
Returning requires **stillness**.

That is why many leaders talk about presence—***but rarely practice return.***

Because return costs time.
It costs slowing down.
It costs letting go of urgency—*even briefly.*

And urgency feels responsible.
Stillness feels risky.

THE SHAME THAT KEEPS LEADERS FROM RETURNING

Many leaders hesitate to return because of quiet shame.

They think:

"I should know better."
"I preach this."
"I teach others to do this."

So instead of returning, they compensate.
They ***work harder***.
They ***push through***.
They ***add activity to cover absence***.

But God does not shame His servants for drifting.

He invites them home.

Return is not an *admission of failure*.
It is an **act of humility**.

RETURNING IS NOT ABOUT DOING — IT IS ABOUT BEING

Returning to presence is not about *adding spiritual disciplines.*

It is about **reclaiming relationship**.

It is not:
Praying longer.
  Reading more.
    Trying harder.

It is:
Being honest.
  Being still.
    Being receptive.

Presence is not earned.
  It is entered.

And the doorway is always humility.

WHY STILLNESS FEELS UNCOMFORTABLE

Stillness feels uncomfortable because it **removes distraction**.

And distraction protects leaders from:

- Feeling disappointment
- *Acknowledging fatigue*
- Facing unresolved grief
- *Naming lost joy*

Noise keeps us functional.
Stillness makes us aware.

But awareness is the beginning of healing.

God does not meet us in pretense.
He meets us in truth.

THE PRODIGAL'S RETURN WAS ABOUT PRESENCE, NOT PERFORMANCE

The prodigal did not return with a plan to prove himself.

He returned empty-handed.

He didn't offer productivity.

He offered honesty.

And the father did not respond with conditions.

He responded with celebration.

Return has always been about **relationship**—not **resume**.

HOW TO RETURN WITHOUT PRESSURE

Returning to presence does not require a retreat.
It does not *demand a sabbatical*.
It does not **wait for ideal conditions**.

It begins with small, faithful steps:

- Sitting quietly before God
- *Opening Scripture without agenda*
- Worshiping without leading
- *Praying without words*

Presence grows where pressure is removed.

WHY GOD DOES NOT RUSH RETURN

God is never in a hurry to restore presence.
He is *patient*.

He allows return to unfold gently—because healing is *fragile*.

He does not overwhelm.
He invites.

Joy returns slowly—not because God withholds it—

... but because **the soul must relearn safety**.

THE MOMENT GOD HAS BEEN WAITING FOR

God has not been waiting for your perfection.
He has been waiting for your attention.

Not more sermons.
Not better leadership.
Not greater sacrifice.

Just you.

Returning to presence is the simplest—*and bravest*—act a leader can make.

A PRACTICE FOR THIS CHAPTER

Before moving on, pause.

Sit quietly.
Do not plan.
Do not evaluate.
Do not prepare.

Simply acknowledge:

"God, I'm here."

That is return.

THE PROMISE OF THIS CHAPTER

Return is always possible.
Presence is always available.

Joy is always closer than you think.

God has not withdrawn.
He has been waiting.

And when presence is reclaimed, *joy begins to rise again.*

> **Because ministry—**
> is way (way, way) too good not to enjoy it.

— 14 —

RELEARNING HOW TO
ENJOY GOD

Most leaders know how to serve God.
Many know how to obey God.
Far fewer remember how to enjoy Him.

Enjoying God can feel *almost foreign* to long-serving
leaders.

Not because they stopped loving Him—but because
ministry *slowly trained them* to relate to God
primarily through **responsibility**.

God became the *One you worked for.*
The *One you consulted.*
The *One you depended on.*

But somewhere along the way, **He stopped being
the One you delighted in**.

And joy cannot survive *where delight is forgotten.*

HOW ENJOYMENT GETS LOST IN MINISTRY

Leaders rarely stop enjoying God intentionally.

They stop gradually.

Enjoyment gets crowded out by:

- *Urgency*
- Responsibility
- *Familiarity*
- Performance

You don't *stop believing God is good.*
You just stop *experiencing Him as enjoyable.*

Time with God becomes *purposeful* rather than
pleasurable.
Scripture becomes **instructional** rather than
relational.
Prayer becomes *necessary* rather than *desired*.

And over time, leaders forget that God is not only
worthy of obedience—***He is worthy of delight***.

WHY ENJOYING GOD CAN FEEL UNPRODUCTIVE

Enjoyment feels unproductive.

There's no *checklist*.
No *measurable outcome*.
No *immediate application*.

And ministry cultures often reward **productivity more than pleasure**.

So, leaders feel subtle guilt when they linger.
They feel pressure to "use the time wisely."
They feel the need to justify enjoyment with usefulness.

But God never demanded *justification for delight*.

David said,

"I will delight myself in the Lord."

Not because it was strategic.
Not because it was efficient.
But because it was right.

ENJOYMENT IS NOT EMOTIONALISM

Enjoying God is not chasing feelings.

It is not hype.
It is not constant excitement.
It is not emotional excess.

Enjoyment is attentive affection.

It is noticing God.
   Appreciating God.
      Receiving God.

Some moments are *joyful*.

Others are *quiet*.
Others are *peaceful*.

Enjoyment is not loud—***it is alive***.

WHY LEADERS FEAR ENJOYMENT

Some leaders fear enjoying God because *enjoyment* feels *vulnerable*.

Enjoyment opens the heart.
It softens defenses.
It invites dependence.

And dependence *can feel risky* to leaders who have learned to be *strong for others*.

But enjoyment is not weakness.
It is trust.

Enjoying God means believing He is good enough to be ***enjoyed***—not just ***endured***.

JESUS ENJOYED THE FATHER

Jesus did not merely *obey the Father*.
He *delighted in Him*.

He spoke of the Father with affection.
He rejoiced in the Spirit.
He withdrew to be alone with God—not out of *duty*, but *desire*.

If Jesus enjoyed His relationship with the Father, **leaders are not less spiritual for wanting the same**.

Enjoyment is not childish.
It is Christlike.

THE DIFFERENCE BETWEEN KNOWING ABOUT GOD AND KNOWING GOD

Leaders know a great deal *about* God.

Attributes.
Doctrine.
Theology.
Truth.

But enjoyment flows from *knowing God*, not just knowing facts *about Him*.

Information can *increase competence.*
Only intimacy *produces joy.*

And intimacy cannot be rushed.

HOW TO RELEARN ENJOYMENT

Relearning how to enjoy God is less about *effort* and more about *permission*.

Permission to:

- Linger without agenda

- Read Scripture slowly
- Sit in silence
- Notice beauty
- Laugh in God's presence

Enjoyment grows where pressure is removed.

It often returns first in small moments:

A phrase in Scripture that *warms the heart.*
A quiet sense of *nearness.*
A moment of gratitude that *feels genuine.*

These moments are not distractions.

They are restorations.

WHY JOY OFTEN RETURNS BEFORE ENERGY

Leaders are often surprised that joy returns before energy.

They expect strength first.
But God often restores delight before stamina.

Joy is not the result of being rested.
Joy is the means by which strength returns.

Delight reawakens the soul.
And the soul fuels the body.

A GENTLE QUESTION FOR THIS CHAPTER

Ask yourself:

When was the last time I simply enjoyed God—
without needing anything from Him?

Not answers.
Not solutions.
Not direction.

Just God.

If it's been a while, that's not failure.
It's an invitation.

THE PROMISE OF THIS CHAPTER

God has not changed.
His goodness has not diminished.
His presence has not become dull.

Enjoyment is not lost forever.
It has just been neglected.

And what has been neglected **can be recovered**.

As leaders relearn how to enjoy God, joy begins to
flow naturally back into ministry.

Because MINISTRY—
    is way too good not to enjoy it.

15

REDISCOVERING THE PRIVILEGE OF PEOPLE

Ministry is about people.

That sounds obvious—*almost too obvious to say.*

And yet, one of the quiet tragedies of long-term ministry is that people can slowly stop *feeling like a privilege* and start *feeling like pressure.*

Not because leaders stop caring.
But because caring costs.

And when joy thins, people often bear the weight of it.

WHEN PEOPLE SHIFT FROM CALLING TO BURDEN

Early in ministry, *people feel like miracles.*

Every conversation matters.
Every story moves you.

Every changed life feels sacred.

You marvel that God would trust you with people's lives.

But over time—especially after wounds, conflict, betrayal, or fatigue—*something can shift.*

People begin to feel:

Demanding instead of **delightful**.
Interruptive instead of **sacred**.
Draining instead of **dignifying**.

And leaders feel guilty for feeling that way.

But guilt doesn't restore joy.
It only deepens the disconnect.

HOW PAIN CHANGES PERCEPTION

Leaders don't stop loving people *because of apathy.*
They stop enjoying people *because of pain.*

Pain from:

- Betrayal
- *Criticism*
- False assumptions
- *Unresolved conflict*
- Unmet expectations

When pain goes *unprocessed*, it reshapes

perception.

People become *potential threats* instead of *sacred trusts.*
Interactions feel *heavy* instead of *holy.*

And joy slips away.

JESUS NEVER LOST SIGHT OF THE INDIVIDUAL

Crowds followed Jesus—*but He never lost sight of individuals.*

He noticed the woman touching His garment.
He called Zacchaeus by name.
He restored Peter privately.
He wept over Jerusalem.

Jesus did not reduce people to problems—*even when they caused pain.*

He remained present.

And His joy flowed from love—*not convenience.*

WHEN LEADERS START MANAGING PEOPLE INSTEAD OF LOVING THEM

Management is necessary in ministry.
But it cannot replace relationship.

When leaders are depleted:

- *People feel like tasks*
- Conversations feel transactional
- *Care feels obligatory*

And leaders grieve the loss of joy—**but don't know how to recover it**.

Joy does not return by *minimizing people*.
It returns by *re-humanizing them*.

THE DANGEROUS LIE: "I CARE TOO MUCH"

Some leaders say, *"I care too much."*

But the problem is rarely caring too much.
The problem is **caring without replenishment**.

Jesus cared deeply—*but He also withdrew*.
He loved fully—*but He also rested*.

Caring becomes heavy when it is **disconnected from presence**.

REDISCOVERING PEOPLE AS SACRED TRUSTS

People are not interruptions to ministry.
They are the ministry.

Every conversation *carries eternity*.
Every prayer *matters*.
Every shepherding moment is *holy ground*.

Joy returns when leaders remember:

These are not **obligations**.
They are **privileges**.

THE PRACTICE OF SEEING PEOPLE AGAIN

Relearning to enjoy people *requires intention*.

It means:

- *Slowing down enough to listen*
- Looking people in the eye
- *Remembering names and stories*
- Celebrating small wins
- *Refusing to let wounds define perception*

Seeing people as sacred again *restores joy gradually*.

A MOMENT OF HONEST REFLECTION

Ask yourself:

When did people start feeling heavy to me?

What pain changed the way I see them?

What would it look like to let God heal that place?

God does not ask you to pretend.

He invites you to heal.

THE PROMISE OF THIS CHAPTER

People can become a source of joy again.

Not because they change.
But because your heart is renewed.

God still loves people passionately.
And when leaders share His heart, *joy flows naturally.*

Because ministry—
   is way too good not to ENJOY it.

16

RECLAIMING WONDER

Wonder is the *soil* where *joy grows*.

When wonder disappears, **joy soon follows**.

Ministry can survive without wonder for a season—
but it cannot thrive.

Without wonder, **leadership** becomes *mechanical*,
obedience becomes *routine*, and **service** becomes
survival.

Reclaiming wonder is not sentimental nostalgia. **It
is spiritual necessity.**

WHY WONDER IS ALWAYS THE FIRST CASUALTY

Wonder dies quietly.

It is crowded out by *familiarity*.
It is dulled by *repetition*.
It is suffocated by *urgency*.

Leaders do holy things so often that holiness can feel ordinary.

Miracles become *expected*.
Answered prayers become *assumed*.
Transformation becomes part of the *job description*.

But heaven never treats transformation casually.

What is routine to us is **still miraculous to God**.

THE DANGEROUS COST OF LOSING WONDER

When wonder fades:

- *Joy thins*
- Gratitude weakens
- *Compassion narrows*
- Cynicism grows

Leaders stop being amazed by what once made them weep.

They stop pausing.
Stop noticing.
Stop celebrating.

And joy quietly *slips away*.

MOSES AND THE BURNING BUSH

Moses had seen *many fires in the desert*.

But one fire made him stop.

The bush burned—but was **not consumed**.

And Moses turned aside.

God spoke when Moses noticed.

Wonder *begins with attention.*

God often waits for leaders to turn aside before He speaks again.

WHY LEADERS STOP TURNING ASIDE

Leaders stop turning aside because they are *in a hurry*.

Schedules are full.
Needs are urgent.
Responsibilities are heavy.

Turning aside feels inefficient.

But wonder *does not happen in haste.*

Wonder requires *margin.*
Margin requires *intention.*

JESUS NEVER LOST HIS WONDER

Jesus *marveled* at faith ... *rejoiced* in the Spirit ... *gave thanks* repeatedly.

Even knowing the Father intimately, He **never treated the miraculous as mundane**.

Closeness did not breed contempt.
It deepened awe.

Joy flowed from that awe.

RECLAIMING WONDER IS A PRACTICE

Wonder does not return automatically.
It must be cultivated.

Practices that restore wonder:

- *Naming what God is doing out loud*
- Celebrating small victories
- *Testifying regularly*
- Slowing down long enough to notice grace

Wonder grows where *gratitude is expressed.*

WHY JOY RETURNS WITH WONDER

Joy thrives on amazement.

Amazement that God still calls.
Still heals.
Still redeems.
Still uses broken people.

When leaders are amazed again, *joy becomes*

natural—not forced.

Wonder reconnects the heart to the sacredness of the call.

THE SMALL MIRACLES WE OVERLOOK

Not all miracles are dramatic.

Some are quiet:

- *Faithfulness in hard seasons*
- Healing that takes time
- *Growth that happens slowly*
- Obedience that goes unseen

Wonder returns when leaders learn to **honor the small**.

Heaven celebrates what earth overlooks.

A MOMENT TO PAUSE AND NOTICE

Pause here.

Name one thing God has done recently that **you have not celebrated**.

One moment you *rushed past.*
One grace you *assumed.*
One miracle you *minimized.*

Celebrate it now.

That is wonder returning.

THE PROMISE OF THIS CHAPTER

Wonder is not lost forever.
It has simply been neglected.

And what is neglected can be reclaimed.

God is still holy.
Ministry is still sacred.
And joy is still available.

Because ministry—

  is WAY too GOOD not to ENJOY it!

17

JOY-FUELED LEADERSHIP

Joy does not weaken leadership.
It strengthens it.

Somewhere along the way, joy was mischaracterized as *softness*—something that might *dull the edge* or *reduce ministry's urgency*. So, leaders learned to lead from *intensity, pressure, and resolve* rather than *delight*.

But Scripture never presents joy as optional decoration for leadership. *It presents joy as fuel.*

When joy returns, leadership does not become careless. ***It becomes clearer.***

THE DIFFERENCE BETWEEN DRIVEN AND DIRECTED LEADERS

Driven leaders *push.*
Joy-fueled leaders *discern.*

Driven leaders *react.*
Joy-fueled leaders *respond.*

Driven leaders *exhaust* themselves and others.
Joy-fueled leaders *create* environments where *life can grow.*

Joyless leadership is often frantic.
Joy-fueled leadership is steady.

Because *joy anchors leaders* in God's sufficiency *instead of their own effort.*

WHY JOY CREATES BETTER DECISION-MAKING

Joy quiets fear.

Fear *rushes* decisions.
Joy *slows* them.

Fear *demands* control.
Joy *allows* trust.

When leaders lack joy, **every decision feels urgent and heavy**.
When joy is present, leaders remember **they are not carrying the future alone**.

Joy *restores* perspective.

Not everything is a crisis.
Not every problem is personal.
Not every setback is permanent.

Joy helps leaders see clearly.

JOY-FUELED LEADERS CREATE HEALTHIER CULTURES

Leaders reproduce what they carry.

Joyless leaders unintentionally create:

- Tense environments
- *Performance-driven cultures*
- Fear of failure
- *Reluctance to rest*

Joy-fueled leaders create:

- Safety
- *Curiosity*
- Creativity
- *Trust*
- Resilience

People do not flourish under pressure alone.
They flourish where joy and purpose coexist.

WHY JOY IN LEADERSHIP IS CONTAGIOUS

Joy spreads.

Not artificial cheerfulness.
Not forced positivity.

But grounded, settled joy.

When leaders enjoy the work God has given them:

- Teams feel permission to breathe
- *Volunteers feel valued*
- Staff feel safe
- *Churches feel alive*

Joy signals *trust.*
Trust invites *participation.*
Participation multiplies *impact.*

JOY CHANGES HOW LEADERS HANDLE CONFLICT

Conflict does not disappear when joy returns.
But the way leaders engage it changes.

Joy allows leaders to:

- *Stay present without being defensive*
- Correct without being harsh
- *Listen without needing to win*

Joy reminds leaders that identity is secure—***even when tension exists.***

Fear-driven leaders *protect themselves.*
Joy-fueled leaders *protect the relationship.*

WHY SOME LEADERS FEAR JOY-FUELED LEADERSHIP

Some leaders fear joy because ***joy feels like letting go.***

They wonder:

"If I relax, will things fall apart?"
"If I enjoy this, will I lose momentum?"
"If I stop pushing, will people stop following?"

But joy does not remove authority.
It removes anxiety.

And anxiety was never meant to be the engine of leadership.

JESUS LED FROM JOY

Scripture tells us **Jesus rejoiced in the Spirit**.

He was *serious* about the mission.
He was *focused* on God's word.
He was *disciplined* for the road ahead.

And yet—**He led from joy**.

Joy did not distract Him from the cross.
It sustained Him toward it.

Joy did not make Him casual.
It made Him secure.

THE PRACTICE OF LEADING
FROM JOY AGAIN

Joy-fueled leadership is not accidental.
It is cultivated.

It requires:

- Regular return to presence
- *Honest acknowledgment of limits*
- Permission to rest
- *Celebration of faithfulness*
- Reframing success through God's eyes

Joy grows where leaders tend their own souls.

A MOMENT OF PERSONAL APPLICATION

Ask yourself:

How has my leadership changed during seasons *when joy was thin*?

How might my leadership change *if joy were restored*?

What environment am I currently creating— *intentionally* or *unintentionally*?

Joy does not just affect how you feel.
It shapes how others experience your leadership.

THE PROMISE OF THIS CHAPTER

Joy-fueled leadership is not naïve.
It is durable.

It does not ignore difficulty.
It outlasts it.

And leaders who lead from joy do not burn out others—*they build them up*.

Because **ministry** ...

... is way too good ...

... not to **enjoy it!!**

18

PROTECTING JOY IN HARD SEASONS

Joy is not fragile—but it is valuable.

And anything valuable must be protected.

Many leaders assume that once joy returns, it will simply stay. *But Scripture never presents joy as something that maintains itself automatically.*

Joy must be guarded, especially in hard seasons.

Because hard seasons are not *exceptions in ministry.* **They are part of it.**

WHY JOY IS MOST VULNERABLE WHEN PRESSURE INCREASES

Pressure exposes **priorities**.

When seasons intensify:

- Schedules tighten
- *Emotions run high*
- Decisions multiply
- *Margin shrinks*

And joy is often the first thing sacrificed in the name of urgency.

Leaders tell themselves:

"I'll enjoy this later."
  "This is just temporary."
    "I don't have time right now."

But temporary seasons often last longer than expected. **And postponed joy is easily lost.**

JOY DOES NOT ELIMINATE PAIN —
IT COEXISTS WITH IT

Joy is not **denial**.

It does not *pretend* pain isn't real.
It does not *ignore* grief.
It does not *minimize* loss.

Joy exists alongside sorrow.

Paul wrote of being "sorrowful, yet always rejoicing." Not *instead of rejoicing*.

Alongside it.

Leaders must *learn to hold both*.

WHY SOME LEADERS LOSE JOY
IN CRISIS

Crises narrow focus.

Everything becomes *urgent*.
Every conversation feels *weighty*.
Every decision feels *critical*.

In crisis, leaders often:

- *Stop resting*
- Stop celebrating
- *Stop noticing God's faithfulness*

They become *reactive*.
They operate in *survival mode*.

Joy disappears not because leaders stop believing—
but because *survival crowds out gratitude*.

THE DISCIPLINE OF NOTICING
GOOD IN HARD TIMES

Protecting joy requires discipline.

Not discipline of denial—but *discipline of attention*.

Attention to:

- *God's presence*
- Small mercies
- *Daily grace*
- Faithful people

- *Quiet victories*

Joy grows where attention is directed.

Leaders who protect joy **deliberately name what God is doing—***even in difficulty*.

BOUNDARIES ARE NOT BARRIERS TO FAITH — THEY ARE GUARDRAILS

Joy requires *margin*.
Margin requires *boundaries*.

Boundaries around:

- *Time*
- Availability
- *Emotional energy*
- Expectations

Boundaries are **not selfish**.
They are **stewardship.**

Leaders who refuse boundaries often lose joy first—
and then effectiveness follows.

WHY JOY NEEDS COMMUNITY

Joy is strengthened in community.

Isolation *weakens joy*.
Connection *reinforces it*.

Leaders need people who:

- *See them*
- Tell them the truth
- *Laugh with them*
- Pray with them
- *Remind them who they are*

Joy fades *faster in isolation.*
It grows **stronger in shared life.**

THE PRACTICE OF REGULAR JOY CHECKS

Wise leaders *check their joy regularly.*

Not to judge themselves.
Not to shame themselves.
But to notice.

Questions like:

"Am I still enjoying this?"
"Where has joy thinned?"
"What has been draining me lately?"

Joy checks prevent erosion.

WHEN JOY NEEDS TO BE DEFENDED

Sometimes joy must be defended against:

- Cynicism

- *Negativity*
- Constant criticism
- *Comparison*
- Overexposure to problems

This does not mean *ignoring reality*. It means **choosing where to dwell mentally and emotionally**.

Joy is not passivity.
It is intentional focus.

A PRACTICE FOR HARD SEASONS

When seasons are hard:

- Shorten your to-do list
- *Lengthen your gratitude list*
- Lower expectations of perfection
- *Raise awareness of grace*

Joy survives where grace is noticed.

THE PROMISE OF THIS CHAPTER

Joy can last—**even in hard seasons**.

Not because circumstances improve.
But because **leaders learn to guard what matters**.

Joy is not accidental.
It is cultivated.

And when joy is protected, ***strength endures***.

Because ministry—

    is way too **OUTSTANDING**

        not to enjoy it!

19

LAUGHING AGAIN WITHOUT GUILT

Somewhere along the way, many leaders *stopped laughing*.

Not because they lost their sense of humor.
Not because life stopped being funny.
But because laughter began to feel ...

... *inappropriate*.

Too *light* for the weight they carry.
Too *casual* for the seriousness of the call.
Too *joyful* for the brokenness they see every day.

So leaders learned to restrain laughter.
To soften smiles.
To keep joy measured and muted.

And guilt quietly replaced gladness.

WHEN LAUGHTER STARTS TO FEEL IRRESPONSIBLE

Many leaders believe—*without ever saying it out loud*—that **laughter signals a lack of seriousness**.

"If I laugh, am I minimizing the pain people are in?"

"If I enjoy this moment, am I being insensitive to suffering?"

"If I smile too freely, will people think I don't care?"

So, leaders carry a constant internal tension:

Joy feels good—*but guilt feels safer*.

However … *guilt is a poor guardian of holiness.*

SCRIPTURE NEVER PORTRAYS JOY AS DISRESPECT

The Bible never treats *joy* as *irreverent*.

It commands rejoicing.
It celebrates gladness.
It describes laughter as gift.

The Psalms speak of **mouths filled with laughter**.

*Ecclesiastes reminds us there is **a time to laugh**.*

Jesus Himself used **humor**, **irony**, and **wit** in His teaching.

Joy was never presented as the *opposite* of compassion. It was presented as ***evidence of trust***.

WHY LAUGHTER IS HEALING, NOT HARMFUL

Laughter heals because it *releases tension.*

It reminds the body it is safe.
It signals the soul it is alive.
It interrupts cycles of heaviness.

For leaders who carry sorrow daily, *laughter is not denial—it is relief.*

It does not erase grief.
It gives the heart space to breathe.

THE DIFFERENCE BETWEEN LEVITY AND LIGHTNESS

There is a difference between *levity* and *lightness.*

Levity *avoids pain.*
Lightness *survives pain.*

Levity *mocks.*
Lightness *restores.*

Healthy laughter does not ***diminish the***

seriousness of ministry. It protects leaders from being **crushed by it**.

WHY SOME LEADERS FEAR BEING SEEN LAUGHING

Leaders are watched.

Words are *interpreted*.
Expressions are *evaluated*.
Moments are *scrutinized*.

So leaders sometimes feel safer **appearing serious than appearing joyful**.

But constant seriousness *does not build trust*.
Authenticity does.

People do not need leaders who *look burdened by God's work*.

They need leaders who show that **walking with God produces life**.

JESUS AND THE JOY OF LIFE

Jesus attended weddings.
Shared meals.
Laughed with friends.

Children ran to Him.
People felt safe with Him.

His joy did not compromise His authority.

It enhanced it.

Joy made Him *approachable*.
It revealed *confidence in the Father*.

THE DAMAGE OF JOYLESS LEADERSHIP

When leaders never laugh:

- *Ministry feels heavy*
- Teams feel tense
- *Faith feels burdensome*

Joyless leadership unintentionally communicates:

"This calling is *exhausting*."
"This life is *draining*."
"This burden is *unbearable*."

But joy-filled leaders quietly say:

"This is hard—*but it's good*."
"This matters—*and it gives life*."
"This walk with God *is worth it*."

RELEARNING TO LAUGH AS A SPIRITUAL PRACTICE

Laughter can be spiritual.

It reminds leaders: ***God is still on the throne***.

The world does not *rest on their shoulders.*
Grace is sufficient.

Laughing again is *not rebellion.*
It is trust.

Trust that God is big enough to handle the weight—
so you don't have to carry it alone.

A GENTLE CHALLENGE IN THIS CHAPTER

Ask yourself:

When did I start feeling guilty for enjoying moments of joy?

Who taught me that laughter and leadership were incompatible?

What would it look like to let joy be visible again?

God is not offended by your laughter.
He delights in it.

THE PROMISE OF THIS CHAPTER

You are allowed to laugh.

You are allowed to **enjoy moments**.
You are allowed to **smile freely**.
You are allowed to **experience delight**.

Joy does not make you less spiritual.

It makes you human—and *humanity was God's design*.

Because ministry—is way too

EXCELLENTLY good not to

enjoy it.

20

MINISTRY IS STILL HOLY GROUND

It may not feel like it used to.

The hours are longer now.
The stakes feel higher.
The weight is heavier.

You've seen too much **to be naïve**.
You've carried too much **to be casual**.
You've stayed too long to pretend it **hasn't cost you something**.

And yet—

Ministry is still holy ground.

Not because it's easy.
Not because it's glamorous.
Not because it always feels rewarding.

But because *God is still here.*

HOLY GROUND DOESN'T ALWAYS LOOK IMPRESSIVE

When Moses encountered holy ground, *it was not in a temple.*

It was a desert.
A bush.
An ordinary place.

Nothing about it looked sacred—*until God revealed Himself.*

Holy ground is not defined by appearance.
It is defined by presence.

And ministry—ordinary, exhausting, complicated ministry ...

... is still saturated with the presence of God.

WHY IT'S EASY TO FORGET THE GROUND IS HOLY

Familiarity dulls awareness.

You've preached the Scriptures *so many times.*
Prayed with *so many people.*
Stood in *so many sacred moments.*

And repetition can rob reverence.

The holy becomes common—not because it is, but because *we've seen it so often.*

But heaven has never grown bored with redemption. *Heaven has never grown tired of restoration.* Heaven has never stopped rejoicing when one life is changed.

The ground is still holy—***even if you've been standing on it a long time***.

THE MOMENT GOD SAID "TAKE OFF YOUR SANDALS"

God told Moses to remove his sandals—not because *the dirt was special*, but because *awareness was required*.

Removing sandals meant slowing down.
It meant recognizing the moment.
It meant honoring what God was doing *right there*.

Leaders often rush past holy ground because they are busy standing on it.

Joy returns when leaders pause long enough to recognize:

"This moment matters."
"This person matters."
"This calling matters."

MINISTRY IS STILL A FRONT-ROW SEAT TO MIRACLES

You still stand where prayers are whispered ... confessions are made ... hearts are softened.

Lives are changed.

You still watch God do things *only He can do.*

You are present at moments angels *lean in to observe.*

That is not ordinary. **That is holy.**

WHY JOY AND HOLINESS BELONG TOGETHER

Holiness is not heaviness.

Holiness is otherness—***the awareness that God is near.***

And joy is the natural response to God's nearness.

When holiness is reduced to seriousness alone, ***joy disappears.***

But when holiness is recognized as God-with-us, ***joy returns.***

Joy does not cheapen the sacred. **It honors it.**

YOU WERE NEVER CALLED TO ENDURE HOLY GROUND

God never said to Moses:

"Brace yourself—this is holy ground."

He said:

"Pay attention."

Ministry is not something to survive.
It is something to steward with reverence and joy.

Yes, it will cost you.
Yes, it will stretch you.
Yes, it will break your heart at times.

But it will also:
Shape you.
    Heal you.
        Fill you.
            Renew you.

Because God meets people on holy ground—**and
you are standing there**.

A FINAL WORD TO THE LEADER
WHO STAYED

You stayed when it was hard.
You stayed when it was thankless.
You stayed when joy thinned and the weight grew
heavy.

This book was never meant to shame you.
It was written to remind you.

To remind you that:

Joy can return.

Wonder can be reclaimed.
Presence can be rediscovered.
Strength can be renewed.

Because God is still calling.
Still speaking.
Still moving.

And ministry—
is still holy ground.

THE LAST INVITATION

Before you close this book, pause.

Take a breath.

Look again at where you are standing.

This place.
   This season.
      This calling.

It is holy ground.

And it is way—
   too good not to enjoy **today**, **tomorrow**, and the
   rest of your life.

A CLOSING PRAYER

Lord,

Open our eyes again.

Where familiarity dulled wonder, restore awe.

Where weight silenced joy, release delight.

Help us stand on holy ground with gratitude, humility, and joy.

Let us serve You not just faithfully—but joyfully.

In Jesus' name,
Amen.

A FINAL WORD

You can find Tim on the South Texas District website at www.stxag.org, on Facebook, or at his Houston office when he's not traveling his home state ministering in the churches across the South Texas District.

He'd be thrilled to connect with you and share stories of God's faithfulness.

www.ingramcontent.com/pod-product-compliance
Lightning Source LLC
Chambersburg PA
CBHW052007090426
42741CB00008B/1583